ROSA
PARKS

and the Montgomery Bus Boycott

by Teresa Celsi

Gateway Civil Rights
The Millbrook Press
Brookfield, Connecticut

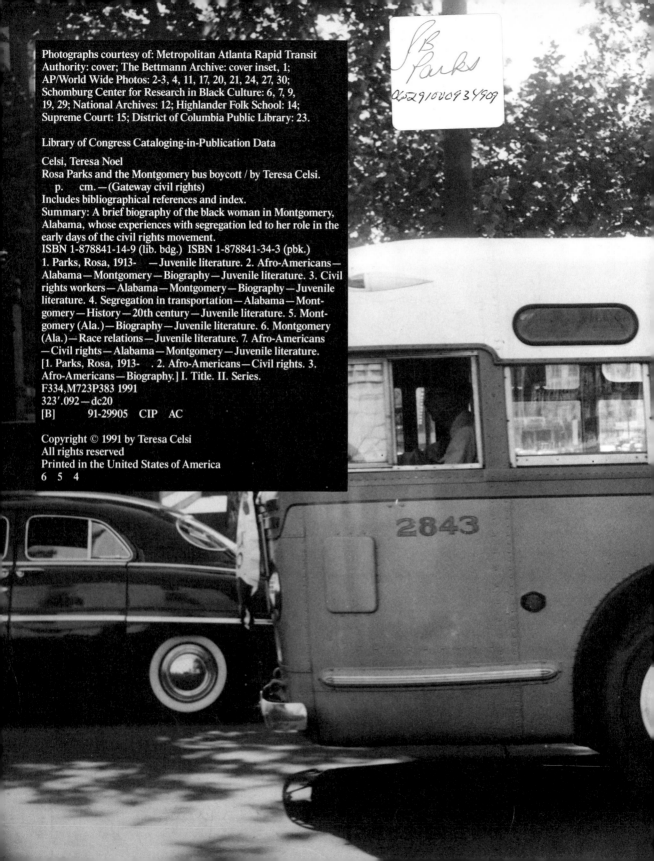

Photographs courtesy of: Metropolitan Atlanta Rapid Transit
Authority: cover; The Bettmann Archive: cover inset, 1;
AP/World Wide Photos: 2-3, 4, 11, 17, 20, 21, 24, 27, 30;
Schomburg Center for Research in Black Culture: 6, 7, 9,
19, 29; National Archives: 12; Highlander Folk School: 14;
Supreme Court: 15; District of Columbia Public Library: 23.

Library of Congress Cataloging-in-Publication Data

Celsi, Teresa Noel
Rosa Parks and the Montgomery bus boycott / by Teresa Celsi.
    p.   cm. — (Gateway civil rights)
Includes bibliographical references and index.
Summary: A brief biography of the black woman in Montgomery,
Alabama, whose experiences with segregation led to her role in the
early days of the civil rights movement.
ISBN 1-878841-14-9 (lib. bdg.) ISBN 1-878841-34-3 (pbk.)
1. Parks, Rosa, 1913-   —Juvenile literature. 2. Afro-Americans—
Alabama—Montgomery—Biography—Juvenile literature. 3. Civil
rights workers—Alabama—Montgomery—Biography—Juvenile
literature. 4. Segregation in transportation—Alabama—Mont-
gomery—History—20th century—Juvenile literature. 5. Montgomery (Ala.)—Biography—Juvenile literature. 6. Montgomery
(Ala.)—Race relations—Juvenile literature. 7. Afro-Americans
—Civil rights—Alabama—Montgomery—Juvenile literature.
[1. Parks, Rosa, 1913-   . 2. Afro-Americans—Civil rights. 3.
Afro-Americans—Biography.] I. Title. II. Series.
F334,M723P383 1991
323′.092—dc20
[B]   91-29905   CIP   AC

Empty buses rolled through the streets of Montgomery during the bus boycott.

Sometimes, great movements can grow out of very small actions. One day, a woman named Rosa Parks was riding on a bus. She was tired, so she sat down. Then the bus driver told her she had to give her seat to someone else—just because that person's skin was white and hers was black. Rosa Parks refused. That one moment changed the history of blacks in this country.

Who was Rosa Parks? Why did she refuse to give up her seat? How did such a little thing become so important?

Growing Up

When Rosa was a little girl, she was afraid to sleep at night. She was born in 1913, at a time when black people in the South often lived in fear. Rosa McCauley (as Rosa Parks was named then) lived with her mother, brother, and grandparents. They all lived on a small farm in Pine Level, Alabama, near the city of Tuskegee. Although the farm was small, it grew enough food to feed them all. Rosa worked in the fields with her grandfather, helping him tend the crops. The days were warm and good.

But the nights were different. At night, groups of white men would ride horses through small southern towns, shooting guns to scare the black residents. These men called themselves the Ku Klux Klan.

Rosa's grandfather was not afraid of the Ku Klux Klan. When he heard the Klan riding in the night, he was ready. He kept a shotgun loaded by the door. But whenever little Rosa heard the galloping horses, she was afraid.

Rosa Parks fought for civil rights for all Americans.

Even movie houses were segregated in the South.

At that time, the schools in the South were segregated. That meant that white children and black children were not allowed to go to the same school. Rosa and her brother went to a school where their mother taught. She was the only teacher. Classes were held in a small church.

When Rosa was 11 years old, she went to a private school for black girls in Montgomery, Alabama. Not many blacks were able to get a good education, but Rosa's mother wanted her daughter to be special. She had saved money for years for Rosa's schooling. There were free public schools in Montgomery, but Rosa was not allowed to attend them. Those schools were for whites only.

"Whites only" was something that Rosa would hear for most of

The Ku Klux Klan

The Ku Klux Klan, or KKK, is a group that first came together at the end of the Civil War. Many white people lost their homes during the Civil War. Families lost brothers, sons, and fathers. Because slavery was one of the reasons that the Civil War was fought, many white people blamed blacks for their troubles. Southern whites could not make blacks slaves again, but they could scare them. If people were scared enough, they would not try to learn. They would not buy property or try to vote.

The KKK had a plan to scare people. They put on white robes and white hoods that hid their faces. They galloped on horseback past black people's homes in the dark of night, firing shotguns. Sometimes they beat blacks. Sometimes they burned down houses and churches. Sometimes they simply left a burning cross in front of someone's house. A burning cross meant that they wanted to kill someone in the house. Often, they did kill that person later on.

Things are different today. The KKK is smaller than it used to be and much less powerful. But it still exists—even today.

Members of the Ku Klux Klan wore robes and hoods to hide their identity and make themselves look frightening.

her life. She could not drink at a public water fountain that said "whites only." She could not buy a meal in a restaurant or see a show in a theater that was for "whites only." She could not ride in the first elevator to be installed in Montgomery. That elevator was for "whites only."

When Rosa was 19 years old, she fell in love with Raymond Parks, and they got married. Now she was no longer Rosa McCauley. She was Rosa Parks. Three years later, she finally finished high school. It had taken many years, but at last she had gotten an education. She felt special, just as her mother had wanted.

Riding the Bus

Ten years after her graduation, Rosa did not feel so special. She felt beaten and tired. Even with a high school education, Rosa could only get work sewing. She worked for a while sewing for people at her home. Then she found a job as a seamstress in the dressmaking section of a department store.

At the end of each long day of work, Rosa had to take a bus ride home. In Montgomery, the buses were segregated. Blacks and whites were not allowed to sit together. The front of the bus was for "whites only." But if the white seats were filled, and a white person got on the bus, the driver would often instruct a black person to stand so that the white person could sit down. In fact, as many as four blacks had to stand if a white person wanted to sit, because blacks and whites could not even sit in the same row together.

Blacks had to sit in the back of the bus.

Also, blacks were often not allowed to walk through the front section of the bus. They had to pay the driver, then step off the bus and come in again through the back door. This seemed very stupid to Rosa, especially when she was tired. One day in 1943, she tried to go through the front section of the bus. The driver, James Blake, told her to get off and go through the back door. When she stepped off the bus he drove away, leaving her standing at the bus stop without her fare.

Rosa was not the only person who was treated badly by a bus driver. Once, a bus was passing by a hospital when a young black soldier stepped out into the street. The bus driver had to brake to keep from hitting him. That made the driver mad. He stepped out of the bus and beat the young soldier in the face with his metal ticket punch.

Although the people on the bus could see this, they were afraid to stop the driver. The same rules that allowed a white person to sit down while a black person had to stand or kept a black person from using a "whites only" water fountain allowed a white person to hit a black person without getting into trouble. The people on the bus knew that if they tried to stop the bus driver, they might be sent to jail. Even if the bus driver had killed the soldier, he probably would not have been punished. As it happened, the young soldier was so badly beaten that he had to go to the hospital.

When Rosa Parks heard about this, she was furious. She decided that she had to do something to change the way black people were treated. She had heard about a group called the National Association for the Advancement of Colored People (the NAACP). The NAACP worked to win black Americans their rights. Rosa Parks decided to join the group.

Working for Equality

When Rosa joined the NAACP, she met a man named Edgar Daniel Nixon. Everyone called him E. D. Nixon. He was the president of the Alabama branch of the NAACP.

E. D. Nixon was very impressed with Rosa Parks. Rosa had learned to type, and she was a good writer, but she had never been allowed to use these skills in a job. E. D. Nixon asked her to be the secretary for the Alabama branch of the NAACP.

At last, Rosa felt special. She was doing important work, and she was doing it well. She wrote letters for the NAACP, set up meetings, and asked important people to speak. She helped many black people register to vote.

One of Rosa's favorite jobs was working with the NAACP's youth group. One time, Rosa took the group to see the Freedom Train. This was a traveling exhibit designed to teach people about the freedoms that exist in America, but when Rosa and the children got to the train, some people

E. D. Nixon

did not want them to go on board. There were many white students from the public schools there. Normally, trains in the South were segregated, so that blacks and whites were not allowed in the same train cars together. But Rosa Parks marched her students right up onto the Freedom Train.

Many of the white teachers were unhappy about this, but the conductors on the train said Rosa's group could go in with the others. After all, the purpose of the train was to show that all Americans had equal rights. Rosa was learning that black people often had to insist upon their rights.

The Freedom Train

The Freedom Train was a real train that traveled around the country in the 1940s. It was a historical exhibit, designed to remind Americans of their heritage. Inside the train were copies of the Declaration of Independence and the Constitution of the United States.

The Declaration of Independence contains the famous phrase "All men are created equal." It states that all people share certain basic rights. The Constitution guarantees these rights to American citizens. One of these rights is the right to free speech. Another is the right to follow the religion of one's choice.

Over the years, other rights have been added to the Constitution. In 1865, the Constitution was changed so that no person could be kept as a slave. In 1870, the right to vote regardless of race or color was added. In 1920, the right to vote was given to women.

The Freedom Train reminded people of these rights. Because of the importance of civil rights to the Constitution, it was decided that the Freedom Train would be open to blacks and whites alike. Under the Constitution, all people are equal, no matter what their race or religion. That was how it was on the Freedom Train, too.

The Constitution of the United States.

Soon after Rosa began working for the NAACP, she started to get strange phone calls. The people who called did not say who they were. They would just yell at her or tell her that they wanted to hurt her. The calls reminded Rosa of the time when she was a little girl and heard the galloping hooves of the Ku Klux Klan in the night. When she was little, she had been afraid. Rosa was still afraid, but now she was angry, too.

Rosa was angry about more than just the phone calls. Other terrible things were happening all around the country. People were getting killed for helping blacks register to vote. One 14-year-old black boy was beaten to death just for teasing a white woman.

Rosa was angry at white people for this and all the other awful things they had done to black people. But she didn't know what to do to change things. And she might never have known if it had not been for her friend Virginia Durr.

Virginia was a white woman. Sometimes Rosa worked for her, doing sewing. Virginia's husband, Clifford, was a lawyer who worked with the NAACP. Although Virginia was white, she was also upset at the way black people were treated. She knew of a place in Tennessee, called the Highlander Folk School, that gave workshops to help people fight segregation. She persuaded Rosa to sign up for classes there.

At first Rosa was afraid. At Highlander, she would be learning alongside white people. She was not used to this because she had never before been to a school that was not segregated. Also, she

Rosa Parks learned how to fight segregation at the Highlander School.

knew that many white people did not like the idea of blacks organizing to fight segregation. She was afraid of what they might do to her. But at last, in the summer of 1955, she decided that she would go.

Rosa had a wonderful time at Highlander. She met people who were fighting segregation all over the country. They all attended workshops together, sharing their stories. Rosa told about going to see the Freedom Train.

After she returned home from Highlander, Rosa did not feel so afraid anymore. She knew now that she was not alone.

Segregated Schools

Until the 1950s, black children and white children in the South did not go to school together. The black children went to separate "colored schools." These schools had very little money. They could not pay teachers much, and they could not afford to buy many books for the students. Classes were often held in churches or in one-room shacks. Often, the schools were not even heated.

Thurgood Marshall was the NAACP lawyer who presented the school segregation case to the Supreme Court. Later, Marshall became the first black justice of the Supreme Court.

Most of the schools for white children were larger. They had more teachers and money to buy new books. In winter, the children sat in heated classrooms. More money was spent to educate white children than black children.

For many years, schools were allowed to remain segregated. Some people tried to fight the laws that said white children and black children had to go to different schools.

Finally, in the 1950s, the NAACP presented a case against segregated schools to the United States Supreme Court. The justices heard the argument and in 1954 made a ruling. They decided that having separate schools for black and white children was unfair to black children. It was a major victory for civil rights.

Rosa Takes a Seat

Not long after Rosa returned from Highlander, she put her new training to use. On Thursday, December 1, 1955, Rosa got on a bus to go home from work. She knew the driver. It was James Blake, the man who had driven away and left her standing on the sidewalk several years before. Rosa paid her fare and sat down. She was not out to make a fuss that day. She was just glad to get a seat.

After a few stops, a white man came onto the bus. James Blake looked back. All the seats were filled. So Blake told the black people in Rosa's row to stand up and let the white man sit down. No one in the row stood up. They were all tired from the long day.

"Y'all make it light on yourselves and let me have those seats," Blake said. The other people in the row finally stood up, but Rosa kept sitting. She had finally decided that she had had enough. She had paid as much as the white man. It was not fair to make her stand.

James Blake started shouting at Rosa to get up. She still refused. Finally, he said he would have her arrested. She told him to go ahead. She was not going to move. At last, Blake went to get a policeman.

Two officers arrived and arrested Rosa. At the police station, she was allowed one phone call. She called her mother. Her mother called E. D. Nixon. He and Clifford and Virginia Durr came to the police station to help. At last, after paying $100 bail, Rosa was allowed to leave.

When they all got home, E. D. Nixon asked Rosa to do something. On Monday, she had to go to court and pay a fine. E. D. Nixon asked her to fight against paying the fine. He told her that people respected her. He said that if she fought against the law that said whites and blacks had to sit in different sections, other blacks would support her. If they all held together, E. D. Nixon said, they might be able to change things.

Rosa Parks was fingerprinted by a policeman after her arrest in Montgomery.

Raymond Parks was afraid of the idea. He did not want Rosa to take a stand. "The white folks will kill you, Rosa!" Raymond cried.

But Rosa had already made her decision. She had made it on the bus when she refused to move. "If you think it will mean something to Montgomery and do some good," Rosa told E. D. Nixon, "I'll be happy to go along with it."

The Boycott Starts

When Rosa said she would fight, E. D. Nixon got busy. He knew a woman named Jo Ann Robinson. She belonged to a group, the Women's Political Council, that was trying to fight the treatment of blacks on the buses. Jo Ann Robinson talked to Nixon that night. She told him that the group had a plan to stop riding the buses.

The next day, Friday, E. D. Nixon called a meeting of the town's black ministers. He wanted the ministers to help him with the plan. E. D. Nixon wanted all of the black people to stop riding the buses on Monday morning. If they could not sit down as the whites could, they would not ride at all. They would boycott the buses.

One of the ministers E. D. Nixon talked to was a young man named Martin Luther King, Jr. King had not lived in Montgomery long, but he was already becoming popular. E. D. Nixon asked him to lead the boycott. King did not know if the boycott would work, but he knew he had to do something. He said yes.

Boycotts

The word "boycott" comes from the name of Captain Charles Boycott. Captain Boycott was an Irish land agent in the 1800s. He worked for a man named Lord Erne. It was Boycott's job to see that the tenants living on Lord Erne's land worked hard. He was very harsh, and the tenants hated him. They decided they would have nothing to do with Boycott or his family. They refused to deal with him. Today, "boycott" means that people refuse to do business with a company because they believe the company is doing something harmful or unfair. Boycotts have been used many times in American history. In recent times, boycotts have been used to protest the poor treatment of migrant farm workers, to protest high prices, and to protest harmful products made by some companies.

These people boycotted Woolworth's stores because they refused to serve blacks.

*Martin Luther King, Jr.,
became a national figure after
the Montgomery bus boycott.*

By the end of the day, thousands of hand-bills—sheets of paper explaining the boy-cott—had been printed. Jo Ann Robinson made the handbills and gave them to child-ren to give out. One of them was given to a man who wrote for a newspaper. The news-paper ran a story about the boycott.

On Sunday, many of the ministers preached special sermons. They spoke about Rosa Parks and how she had refused to give up her seat. They asked everybody not to take the buses on Monday morning.

On Sunday night, though, E. D. Nixon and Martin Luther King, Jr., were worried. What if their plan did not work? What if people did not join the boycott? That might just make things worse!

The next day, Martin Luther King, Jr., was up early. He was still worried. But as he sat down to breakfast, he heard his wife, Coretta, call out, "Come quick, Martin! You have to see this!"

Martin ran to the window and looked out. A bus was just pulling up at the stop outside his house. Usually, the bus was full of people going to work. On this day, though, the bus was completely empty. Martin could not believe it.

He and Coretta watched more buses go by. Sometimes a bus would pull up with a few white people on it, but they did not see one single black person riding on a bus. Martin was filled with joy. The people had stood together. The plan was working.

That morning, Rosa Parks went down to the courthouse. She paid a fine for disobeying the bus driver, but she also brought a lawyer with her. His name was Fred Gray. He told the judge that Rosa would

Rosa was surrounded by well-wishers as she entered the Montgomery courthouse.

appeal her case. The law was unjust, he said, and should be thrown out. When Rosa and Fred Gray stepped out of the courthouse, a crowd of blacks was standing outside waiting for them. They cheered the brave woman who had stood up to the bus driver and the courts.

That night, Martin Luther King, Jr., gave a speech at a special church meeting. So many people came that they could not all fit inside. Several thousand stood outside. King reminded the people how tired they were of being treated unfairly. He asked them to stick together and keep the boycott going. Above all, he urged them to avoid violence. He believed that the best way to fight hatred was not with more hatred, but with love.

The people left the church that night determined to keep the boycott going for as long as the city refused to listen. At first, they asked for very little. They simply wanted the bus company to hire black drivers. They also wanted to change the law so that blacks would not have to give up their seats to white people. And they wanted to be treated politely. It did not seem like much to ask to be treated politely, but the bus company and the city refused even to talk about changing things. Although the bus company was losing money, it did not want to change its rules.

Because the bus company refused these simple requests, the boycotters decided to go further. They demanded that bus segregation be ended completely. Again, the bus company and the city refused to talk about changing things. So, black people in Montgomery continued to walk to work.

This scene from the King Mural in Washington, D.C., shows Rosa Parks during her famous bus ride.

CLEVELAND AVE.

The End of the Boycott

It takes a long time to appeal a law case. For over a year, the black people of Montgomery boycotted the buses. During that time, blacks drove to work in car pools or rode to work on horses or mules. But most of all, they walked. It was like watching a parade each morning to see all the black men and women marching down the streets together.

It was tiring and difficult, but Montgomery's blacks felt right about what they were doing.

Even some of the white people in Montgomery joined the boycott. They helped because they thought the blacks were being treated unfairly. Some of these white people wrote letters to newspapers. Some gave money to help the car pools pay for gas. But some of the

During the boycott, blacks used hearses, mule carts, and just about anything else to get to work.

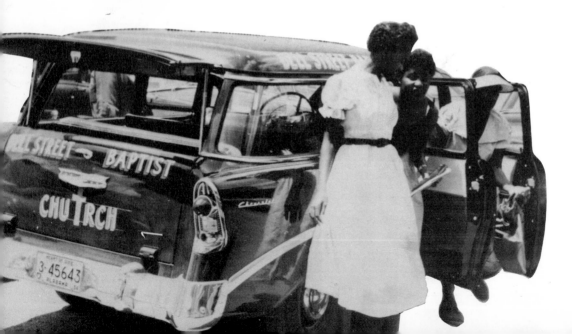

people who gave money asked that their names be kept secret. They were afraid of what other whites might do.

There were good reasons to be afraid. As the boycott continued, the bus company lost so much money that it had to cut back on the number of buses serving the city. This made many white people angry. They blamed the black leaders of the boycott for all the trouble. The Kings' house was bombed. He was not home, but his wife and baby daughter were. Martin was sick with worry until he got home and saw that they were safe.

Finally, 13 months after the boycott started, Rosa's case was settled. The U.S. Supreme Court, the highest court in the nation, ruled that Montgomery's segregation laws were unconstitutional. The Court declared that segregated buses were unfair to black people and that it was illegal to treat people differently because of the color of their skin.

The day after the city's segregation laws were changed, Rosa Parks rode the bus. She proudly took a seat right up front. It had taken more than a year, but she had won.

Rosa had won more than just a fight between one tired woman and one rude bus driver. She had shown that black Americans could stand up for their rights. All the blacks of Montgomery had shown the world that they could stand together. They would fight for their rights together, no matter how long it took. The bus boycott in Montgomery was a battle for civil rights—for equal rights for all. Soon, other civil rights battles would follow.

Afterword

After the boycott was over, Rosa Parks faded from the spotlight of history. She had given up much in the fight. Early in the boycott, she had lost her job in the department store. People had complained about her, and her boss did not want to lose customers. So, after she won her court case, Rosa and her family moved north to Detroit, Michigan.

There, Rosa Parks continued to fight to change things. She worked in the office of John Conyers, a young black congressman. She returned to Alabama briefly to join Martin Luther King, Jr., as he protested against other injustices. She was elected to the board of directors of the NAACP. And, in 1987, she started the Raymond and Rosa Parks Institute for Self-Development, an organization to teach young people how to help themselves and their communities.

In 1988, Rosa appeared at the Democratic National Convention in Atlanta, Georgia. Jesse Jackson, the black leader who was running for president of the United States, presented her to the cheering crowd as the woman whose brave actions had helped start the civil rights movement.

Rosa Parks joined Jesse Jackson at the
1988 Democratic National Convention.

When Rosa was a little girl, her biggest goal had been to get a high school education. She never thought that one day she would help to end segregation. She never dreamed of working for a black congressman, much less standing beside a black candidate for president of the United States. It took the efforts of millions of black Americans to bring about the great changes that occurred during the civil rights movement. But those people might never have had the courage to make those changes if Rosa Parks had not refused to give up her seat on that bus.

Jesse Jackson knew that. That was why he introduced Rosa Parks to the Atlanta Convention with these simple words: ''Rosa Parks. We all stand on her shoulders.''

Important Dates in the Life of Rosa Parks

1913	Rosa McCauley is born on February 4, in Tuskegee, Alabama.
1924	Rosa enters school in Montgomery.
1932	Rosa marries Raymond Parks.
1943	Rosa joins the Alabama NAACP and becomes secretary of the Montgomery branch.
1955	Rosa attends Highlander Folk School in Tennessee. Rosa refuses to give up her seat on a bus, and the Montgomery bus boycott begins.
1956	The U.S. Supreme Court rules that segregation on Montgomery buses is illegal.
1957	Rosa and her family move to Detroit, Michigan.
1988	Rosa appears at the Democratic National Convention in Atlanta, Georgia.

APR · 1959

MACK CHARLES PARKER · TAKEN FR[O]
AND LYNCHED · POPLARVILLE, MS.

· 1957

PRESIDENT EISENHOWER ORDERS
FEDERAL TROOPS TO ENFORCE SCHOO[L]
DESEGREGATION · LITTLE ROCK, AR

1957

CONGRESS PASSES FIRST CIVIL RIGHTS A
SINCE RECONSTRUCTION

[LE]LIE EDWARDS JR · KILLED BY KLAN
[MO]NTGOMERY, AL

SUPREME COURT BANS SEGREGATED
ON MONTGOMERY BUSES

1956

MONTGOMERY BUS BOYCOTT BEG[INS]

· 1955

ROSA PARKS ARRESTED FOR RE[FUSING TO]
GIVE UP HER SEAT ON BUS TO [A WHITE]
MAN · MONTGOMERY, AL

DEC · 1955

Find Out More About Rosa Parks

Books: *Extraordinary Black Americans from Colonial to Contemporary Times* by Susan Altman (Chicago: Childrens Press, 1989).

Rosa Parks by Eloise Greenfield (New York: Crowell, 1973).

The Story of the Montgomery Bus Boycott by R. Conrad Stein (Chicago, Childrens Press, 1986).

Movies: *Eyes on the Prize* is a documentary series that covers the whole civil rights movement.

Places: The Civil Rights Memorial in Montgomery, Alabama, is a tribute to those who died in the struggle for civil rights. It is located in downtown Montgomery, at the corner of Washington and Hull Streets.

The Civil Rights Memorial in Montgomery.

Index